THE EVOLUTION
OF AFRICA'S MAJOR NATIONS

Sudan and Southern Sudan

THE EVOLUTION
OF AFRICA'S MAJOR NATIONS

Sudan and
Southern Sudan

Dorothy Kavanaugh

South Sudan

Sudan

Mason Crest
Philadelphia

Mason Crest
370 Reed Road
Broomall, PA 19008
www.masoncrest.com

CPSIA Compliance Information: Batch #EAMN2013-23. For further information,
contact Mason Crest at 1-866-MCP-Book.

3 5 7 9 8 6 4 2

Library of Congress Cataloging-in-Publication Data

Kavanaugh, Dorothy, 1969-
Sudan / Dorothy Kavanaugh.
    p. cm. — (Evolution of Africa's major nations. East)
Includes bibliographical references and index.
ISBN 978-1-4222-2185-3 (hardcover)
ISBN 978-1-4222-2213-3 (pbk.)
ISBN 978-1-4222-9426-0 (ebook)
1. Sudan—Juvenile literature. I. Title. II. Series: Evolution of Africa's major nations. East.
DT154.6.K385 2012
962.4—dc22
                    2011018502

Table of Contents

Africa: Progress, Problems, and Promise

Robert I. Rotberg

Africa is the cradle of humankind, but for millennia it was off the familiar, beaten path of global commerce and discovery. Its many peoples therefore developed largely apart from the diffusion of modern knowledge and the spread of technological innovation until the 17th through 19th centuries. With the coming to Africa of the book, the wheel, the hoe, and the modern rifle and cannon, foreigners also brought the vastly destructive transatlantic slave trade, oppression, discrimination, and onerous colonial rule. Emerging from that crucible of European rule, Africans created nationalistic movements and then claimed their numerous national independences in the 1960s. The result is the world's largest continental assembly of new countries.

There are 53 members of the African Union, a regional political grouping, and 48 of those nations lie south of the Sahara. Fifteen of them, including mighty Ethiopia, are landlocked, making international trade and economic growth that much more arduous and expensive. Access to navigable rivers is limited, natural harbors are few, soils are poor and thin, several countries largely consist of miles and miles of sand, and tropical diseases have sapped the strength and productivity of innumerable millions. Being landlocked, having few resources (although countries along Africa's west coast have tapped into deep offshore petroleum and gas reservoirs), and being beset by malaria, tuberculosis, schistosomiasis, AIDS, and many other maladies has kept much of Africa poor for centuries.

Thirty-two of the world's poorest 44 countries are African. Hunger is common. So is rapid deforestation and desertification. Unemployment rates are often over 50 percent, for jobs are few—even in agriculture. Where Africa once

Aerial view of Juba, the capital of the newly formed state of South Sudan, with the Nile River flowing past the city.

was a land of small villages and a few large cities, with almost everyone engaged in growing grain or root crops or grazing cattle, camels, sheep, and goats, today more than half of all the more than 1 billion Africans, especially those who live south of the Sahara, reside in towns and cities. Traditional agriculture hardly pays, and a number of countries in Africa—particularly the smaller and more fragile ones—can no longer feed themselves.

There is not one Africa, for the continent is full of contradictions and variety. Of the 750 million people living south of the Sahara, at least 150 million

Women carry water from an irrigation canal back to their village in central Sudan.

live in Nigeria, 85 million in Ethiopia, 68 million in the Democratic Republic of the Congo, and 49 million in South Africa. By contrast, tiny Djibouti and Equatorial Guinea have fewer than 1 million people each, and prosperous Botswana and Namibia each are under 2.2 million in population. Within some countries, even medium-sized ones like Zambia (12 million), there are a plethora of distinct ethnic groups speaking separate languages. Zambia, typical with its multitude of competing entities, has 70 such peoples, roughly broken down into four language and cultural zones. Three of those languages jostle with English for primacy.

Given the kaleidoscopic quality of African culture and deep-grained poverty, it is no wonder that Africa has developed economically and politically less rapidly than other regions. Since independence from colonial rule, weak governance has also plagued Africa and contributed significantly to the widespread poverty of its peoples. Only Botswana and offshore Mauritius have been governed democratically without interruption since independence. Both are among Africa's wealthiest countries, too, thanks to the steady application of good governance.

Aside from those two nations, and South Africa, Africa has been a continent of coups since 1960, with massive and oil-rich Nigeria suffering incessant periods of harsh, corrupt, autocratic military rule. Nearly every other country on or around the continent, small and large, has been plagued by similar bouts of instability and dictatorial rule. In the 1970s and 1980s Idi Amin ruled Uganda capriciously and Jean-Bedel Bokassa proclaimed himself emperor of the Central African Republic. Macias Nguema of Equatorial Guinea was another in that same mold. More recently Daniel arap Moi held Kenya in thrall and Robert Mugabe has imposed himself on once-prosperous Zimbabwe. In both of those cases, as in the case of Gnassingbe Eyadema in Togo and the late Mobutu Sese Seko in Congo, these presidents stole wildly and drove entire peoples and their nations into penury. Corruption is common in Africa, and so are a weak rule-of-law framework, misplaced development, high expenditures on soldiers and low expenditures on health and education, and a widespread (but not universal) refusal on the part of leaders to work well for their followers and citizens.

Conflict between groups within countries has also been common in Africa. More than 12 million Africans have been killed in civil wars since 1990, while another 9 million have become refugees. Decades of conflict in Sudan led to a January 2011 referendum in which the people of southern Sudan voted overwhelmingly to secede and form a new state. In early 2011, anti-government protests spread throughout North Africa, ultimately toppling long-standing regimes in Tunisia and Egypt. That same year, there were serious ongoing hostilities within Chad, Ivory Coast, Libya, the Niger Delta region of Nigeria, and Somalia.

Despite such dangers, despotism, and decay, Africa is improving. Botswana and Mauritius, now joined by South Africa, Senegal, Kenya, and Ghana, are beacons of democratic growth and enlightened rule. Uganda and Senegal are taking the lead in combating and reducing the spread of AIDS, and others are following. There are serious signs of the kinds of progressive economic policy changes that might lead to prosperity for more of Africa's peoples. The trajectory in Africa is positive.

Fertile land, desert, grasslands, and swamp can all be found in Sudan. (Opposite) A field of sorghum, a type of grain, grows in the Nuba Mountains of Sudan. (Right) Some Sudanese still use camels for transportation across the country's desert.

The Land and Climate

AHLAN WA SAHLAN! That's how residents of northern Sudan might greet a visitor to their country, using an Arabic phrase that means "welcome, make yourself at home." Arabic is the official language of Sudan, a country located in northern Africa, south of Egypt. Sudan's other neighbors include Libya to the northwest, Chad and the Central African Republic to the west, and Ethiopia and Eritrea to the east.

Sudan's neighbor to the south is the newest country in Africa, the Republic of South Sudan. From 1956 until early 2011, this territory was part of Sudan. However, the people of the South are ethnically and religiously different from the people of northern Sudan. The differences led to decades of civil war in Sudan, fought mainly during two periods (1955-1972 and 1983-2005) in which an estimated 2.5 million people, mostly civilians, died.

A comprehensive peace agreement to end the fighting was finally signed in January 2005. As part of this agreement, the south was granted a six-year period of autonomy as part of Sudan. This was to be followed by a referendum, or public vote, to determine whether the region would remain part of Sudan or break away to form an independent state. In January 2011, the people of South Sudan voted overwhelmingly in favor of secession. Independence was attained on July 9, 2011.

SUDAN: WEATHER AND CLIMATE

The Republic of Sudan is located north of the equator, in a region known as the Torrid Zone. This area is between the Tropic of Cancer in the northern hemisphere and the Tropic of Capricorn in the southern hemisphere. The Torrid Zone receives more direct sunlight than any other part of the earth. As a result, the heat in Sudan can be oppressive.

Because Sudan is located in the tropics, temperatures are hot all year long. In the capital city of Khartoum, where most of the country's population is clustered, temperatures often surpass 100° Fahrenheit (38° Celsius) during the summer. The high humidity in the city makes the heat even harder to bear. Temperatures in the desert can climb to 110°F (43°C) in the summer, although on a winter night they may drop as low as 40°F (4°C).

Annual rainfall in desert regions of Sudan, which are mainly in the north and west, can be as little as 0.08 inches (0.2 centimeters). Direct sunlight and hot winds have dried out the soil in Sudan's desert areas, making it incapable of trapping the little rainfall that occurs, so virtually

THE GEOGRAPHY OF SUDAN

Location: Northern Africa, bordering the Red Sea, between Egypt and Eritrea

Area: (slightly larger than Alaska)
  total: 718,723 square miles (1,861,484 sq km)

Borders: Central African Republic, 109 miles (175 km); Chad 845 miles (1,360 km); Egypt, 791 miles (1,275 km); Eritrea, 376 miles (605 km); Ethiopia, 448 miles (769 km); Libya, 238 miles (383 km); South Sudan 1,357 miles (2,184 km)*; coastline, 530 miles (853 km)

Climate: hot and dry; arid desert; rainy season varies by region (April to November)

Terrain: generally flat, featureless plain; desert dominates the north

Elevation extremes:
  lowest point: Red Sea 0 feet (0 meters)
  highest point: Jabal Marrah 10,076 feet (3,071 meters)

Natural hazards: dust storms and periodic persistent droughts

* Note: Sudan-South Sudan boundary represents January 1, 1956, alignment; final alignment pending negotiations and demarcation; final sovereignty status of Abyei region pending negotiations between Sudan and South Sudan.

Source: CIA World Factbook, 2012.

nothing can grow. In non-desert areas, the rainy season lasts from April to November, with the heaviest rain occurring in August. Khartoum receives an average of 6.5 inches (16.4 cm) of rain each year. The central part of Sudan receives about 16 inches (40 cm) of rain a year

One climate problem in Sudan is the regular occurrence of dust storms known as *haboobs*. These are caused by strong winds that originate to the north, in the Sahara Desert of Libya and Egypt. During these storms, which typically sweep across the Republic of Sudan between May and July, a wall of dust may totally block out the sun. *Haboobs* can last three or four days,

This satellite photo shows an enormous dust storm blowing out of Sudan across the Red Sea.

making travel impossible. Sudan is one of the few countries in the world that experiences these storms.

SOUTH SUDAN: WEATHER AND CLIMATE

South Sudan also has a tropical climate. In July, the coolest month, average temperatures are typically between 68° and 86°F (20° and 30°C). Average temperatures in March, the warmest month, range from 73° to 98°F (23° to 37°C).

As in Sudan, the rainy season in South Sudan usually lasts from April to November, with most of the rain falling from May to October. Overall, most of South Sudan, including Juba, the capital, receives about 40 inches (100 cm) of rain a year. The higher rain levels are due in part to moisture-laden winds that blow in from the Congo River Basin to the south. However, if these winds are late in developing, drought and famine can occur. This happens periodically, most recently in 2011.

SUDAN: GEOGRAPHIC FEATURES

Most of Sudan is covered by desert. The Libyan desert in the northwest and the Nubian desert in the north-central part of the country are harsh places where sand dunes and scorpions are plentiful, but rain and vegetation are rare. In the southern part of Sudan, the land turns to flat savanna-type plains. These grasslands are home to giraffes, lions, cheetahs, zebras, antelope, rhinoceros, and leopards.

Although the terrain in Sudan is mostly flat, the country does have several mountain ranges. The Red Sea Hills overlook the Red Sea in the east, while the Marra Mountains tower over Darfur in the western part of the country. This range of volcanic peaks includes Sudan's highest point, which is more than 10,000 feet (3,000 m) above sea level. The Nuba Mountains in the southern part of Sudan house fertile valleys where cotton and *sorghum* are farmed.

Water is precious in the northern and western parts of Sudan. Rich soil suitable for growing crops can only be found in a small strip of land along the Nile River. The Nile is the world's longest river, traveling some 3,470 miles (5,584 kilometers) from Lake Victoria in East Africa through South Sudan and Sudan to Egypt in North Africa. The Nile is actually formed from two rivers: the Blue Nile, which flows across Sudan from Ethiopia, and the White Nile, which enters South Sudan from Uganda. The White Nile is the longer and calmer of the two, but the Blue Nile provides a greater volume of water when the two rivers come together near Khartoum. Crocodiles and hippos live in the rivers.

In western Sudan, where there are no permanent streams or large bodies of fresh water, people and animals cannot venture far from wells or waterholes.

SOUTH SUDAN: GEOGRAPHIC FEATURES

In South Sudan, the terrain gradually rises from the plains of the north and center to southern highlands along the border with Uganda and Kenya. In these forested areas, the soil is quite fertile. However, farming in the country is hampered by periodic droughts as well as soil erosion. Elephants, monkeys, and tropical birds, which live in the forests and jungles

The White Nile River, which flows north out of Central Africa, is the major geographic feature of the country. It provides drinking water for people and animals, a home for fish, a source of electricity, and—when its annual summer flood arrives—rich sediment for growing crops.

River valleys in South Sudan are home to a wide variety of trees, such as acacia, ebony, and baobab. Cotton, papyrus, rubber, and castor-oil plants are also *indigenous* to the Nile basin. Animals that live in South Sudan include gazelles, zebras, antelopes, and black rhinoceros.

The White Nile's source is Lake Victoria in Uganda, Tanzania, and Kenya, some 2,000 miles (3,218 km) from the point where the two Niles come together. In South Sudan the river feeds an enormous swampland called the Sudd. The Sudd (this name comes from the Arabic word *sadd*, meaning "barrier") covers 6,370 square miles (16,492 sq km) during the country's dry season. During the wet summers, it can expand to cover as much as 12,350 square miles (31,974 sq km)—an area the size of the state of Maryland. This enormous marsh area contains dense thickets of papyrus and other plants. At times the vegetation is so thick that the river seems to disappear. The Sudd is frequented by crocodiles, hippos, and other animals, as well as countless species of tropical insects.

The Didinga Hills, Dongotona Mountains, and the Imatong Mountains are among the highest places in South Sudan.

THE GEOGRAPHY OF SOUTH SUDAN

Location: East-Central Africa; south of Sudan, north of Uganda and Kenya, west of Ethiopia.

Area: (slightly smaller than Texas)
total: 248,777 square miles (644,329 sq km)

Borders: Central African Republic 615 miles (989 km), Democratic Republic of the Congo 397 miles (639 km); Ethiopia 580 miles (934 km); Kenya 144 miles (232 km); Sudan 1,357 miles (2,184 km)*; Uganda, 270 miles (435 km).

Climate: hot with seasonal rainfall, which is heaviest in the upland areas of the south and diminishes to the north.

Terrain: rises from plains in the north and center to southern highlands along the border with Uganda and Kenya.

Elevation extremes:
lowest point: Red Sea 0 feet (0 meters)
highest point: Kinyeti 10,456 feet (3,187 meters)

*Sudan-South Sudan boundary represents January 1956 alignment; final alignment pending negotiations and demarcation; final sovereignty status of Abyei region pending negotiations between Sudan and South Sudan.

Source: CIA World Factbook, 2012.

On July 9, 2011, the new country of South Sudan officially seceded from Sudan. (Opposite) Salva Kiir Mayardit, president of the Republic of South Sudan, holds a copy of the interim constitution for his new nation, which he had just signed. (Right) Young Sudanese men ride through Juba in a vehicle carrying the flag of South Sudan on the eve of independence.

2 The History of Sudan

For most of its modern history, Sudan has been a divided land. The Arab and Muslim culture of the north is very different from the tribal culture of the south, and those differences led to almost constant conflict since the country became independent in 1956. In 2011 Sudan was divided along those lines when the Republic of South Sudan became independent. However, suspicion and mistrust on both sides remain, and it remains unknown whether the two countries can coexist peacefully.

ANCIENT HISTORY

Human history in the area of present-day Sudan dates back thousands of years. Ancient Egyptian traders followed the Nile River south into the region, which they called Kush, around 2000 B.C. When they arrived, they found a people called the Nubians who lived along the Nile. The Nubians were farmers, herdsmen, and hunters.

Around the year 1550 B.C., the armies of the Egyptian Pharaoh Ahmose I invaded Kush, conquering the region and making it a province of Egypt. However, Kush eventually grew stronger than Egypt. In the eleventh century B.C. a Nubian society based at the city of Napata regained independence from Egyptian rule. By the eighth century, the Nubians had conquered part of southern Egypt and established the powerful Kingdom of Kush.

The Nubians eventually moved their capital to Meroe, a city on the Nile just north of present-day Khartoum. Meroe's culture was similar to Egypt's in many ways. Pottery and burial *talismans* have been found in Sudan that are older than similar discoveries made in Egypt. This indicates that both civilizations influenced the other. The Nubians built burial pyramids for their rulers; although they are much smaller than the enormous pyramids of Egypt, there are more of them. At one time, the two civilizations had similar languages and religions, but over time these became very different.

Although the Nubians were forced out of Egypt around 670 B.C., the Merotic civilization flourished until the first century B.C. After the Roman Empire conquered Egypt in 30 B.C., a Roman army invaded northern Sudan to stop Nubian raids into Egypt. In 23 B.C., the Romans sacked Meroe, sending the kingdom into a period of decline. About A.D. 350, Meroe was invaded and completely destroyed by the Axumites, a tribe from modern Ethiopia.

The Romans continued to exert a strong influence over the Sudan region for several hundred years. However, Rome itself went into a period of decline during the fourth and fifth centuries. The empire was divided into western

The ancient civilizations of Meroe and Egypt shared several characteristics. For example, the people of Meroe built pyramid tombs to honor their rulers, just as the Egyptians did.

and eastern halves after 395. After Rome, the capital of the eastern empire, fell to barbarians in 476, the eastern (or Byzantine) empire maintained control over Egypt. However, the Byzantines did not have the resources to project their military power south into Nubia. Tribal groups stepped in to fill the power vacuum.

THE ARRIVAL OF ISLAM

By the sixth century, three new kingdoms had emerged in the Sudan region along the Nile: Nobatia, Muqurra, and Alwa. Christianity was the official religion of each state, but each kingdom adhered to a different *sect*. This led to occasional fighting.

By the seventh century, the Africans faced a new enemy. Arab tribes, united by the Prophet Muhammad's new religion, Islam, emerged from the Arabian Peninsula after Muhammad's death in 632. They spread their religion by conquering neighboring territories, such as Persia and Egypt. Perhaps in response to this threat, Nobatia and Muqurra merged into a new, stronger state, the kingdom of Dunqulah.

The Nubians of Dunqulah were able to defeat an Arab army in 652. This led to a peace agreement, known as the *bakt*, which lasted for centuries. Under the *bakt*, the Nubians sent hundreds of slaves to Egypt each year in exchange for food and other goods. Arab language and customs gradually took root, particularly in the north, because the Nubians had to learn Arabic in order to trade with their neighbors. Islam spread gradually through the spread of Arab settlers and Muslim missionaries.

Dunqulah grew weaker after the tenth century. In 1276 the Mamluks, a powerful group of Muslims who ruled Egypt, helped overthrow the king of Dunqulah and placed a new king on the throne. Though Dunqulah remained nominally independent, the Mamluks essentially controlled the state. As Muslims gained power in the region, the Nubian Christian church declined. In 1315 the first Muslim king of Dunqulah took the throne, and by 1500 most people of Dunqulah had converted to Islam. In 1517 the powerful Ottoman Empire absorbed both Egypt and Dunqulah.

To the south, the kingdom of Alwa was also on the decline. Around 1500, the kingdom fell to the Funj, a race of black Africans who practiced Islam. The Funj would continue to rule the southern region until the 19th century. In east Sudan, another small Funj kingdom arose—the kingdom of Sennar, which thrived from the 16th to the 18th centuries.

FOREIGN INVOLVEMENT

By the end of the 18th century, most of Sudan was considered part of Egypt, and thus under Ottoman control. However, European countries were growing interested in North Africa. In 1798, a French army led by Napoleon Bonaparte invaded Egypt. Although the Ottomans, with the help of Great Britain, forced the French to leave in 1801, the region entered a chaotic period.

In 1805, the Ottoman sultan appointed a man named Muhammad Ali to rule Egypt. Once Ali had gained control over the country, he decided to make Egypt independent of the Ottoman Empire. To do this, he would need money and a strong military. In 1820 Ali's forces invaded Sudan, where he hoped to acquire gold and slaves to serve in his army. Within a year, 50,000 Sudanese had been killed and another 30,000 sent north to Egypt as slaves.

The Egyptian invasion marked the start of 60 years of Egyptian rule over Sudan. The Egyptians were harsh rulers. They extracted high taxes and exploited or enslaved the nomadic people of the region. However,

The Egyptian ruler Muhammad Ali invaded Sudan in 1820 and soon brought the region under his control.

under Egyptian rule modern farming and irrigation techniques were introduced, and railroad and telegraph lines were constructed.

Europeans remained interested in Egypt and its Sudan territory. In the 1850s a French company began working on a canal that would connect the Mediterranean Sea with the Red Sea and Indian Ocean. The Suez Canal opened in 1869. For Great Britain, the canal was an important connection to its colony in India. To protect this connection the British became more involved in Egyptian affairs. In 1882 the British took control of Egypt's government, although nominally the country remained part of the Ottoman Empire.

THE MAHDI'S REBELLION

In Sudan, a charismatic Muslim leader named Muhammad Ahmed soon rebelled against British rule. Ahmed was a leader of a fringe Islamic sect called Sammaniyah; he claimed to be the Mahdi, a prophet sent to prepare Muslims for the end of the world. In 1883, the Mahdi called for a holy war (or *jihad*) against Sudan's Egyptian and British occupiers. He achieved a series of impressive military victories, including the defeat of 7,000 Egyptian troops near al-Ubayyid and the massacre of British troops under General Charles Gordon after the 1884–85 siege of Khartoum. After these defeats, the British and Egyptians withdrew from Sudan.

The Mahdi died just five months after the victory at Khartoum. Although he set up a government before he died, over the next few years Sudan became a chaotic place as various leaders fought for power. In 1891, Abdullah ibn Muhammad emerged from the fighting as *khalifa*, or ruler, of Sudan. However, this did not stabilize the country. According to some sources, about half of the population died due to famine, disease, persecution, and warfare between 1885 and 1900.

During the mid-1890s, the British government decided to regain control over Sudan. The major battle occurred at Omdurman, a small city just north of Khartoum where the Mahdi's tomb was located. Although the British were heavily outnumbered, they were armed with machine guns and modern artillery. This turned the battle in their favor; British casualties were 48 dead and 382 wounded, compared to some 10,000 dead, 15,000 wounded, and 5,000 captured on the Sudanese side.

With the *khalifa* defeated, British leaders established the modern borders of Sudan. These borders included two distinctly different regions. Most of the people

The Mahdi's men prepare to kill British general Charles Gordon at Khartoum, 1885.

who lived in northern Sudan were Muslims of Arab descent. Culturally, they were similar to the people of Egypt and other Arab countries. The people of southern Sudan were black African tribesmen, most of whom were Christians or animists. Culturally, they were more like the people of other sub-Saharan African countries. The cultural and religious differences would create tension between the two areas of the country.

THE CONDOMINIUM PERIOD

In 1899 Britain and Egypt agreed to share control of Sudan. Their agreement, called the *condominium*, brought about a relatively prosperous and peaceful period for Sudan. However, decisions made during this time would sow the seeds of eventual discord. The British rulers treated the northern and southern areas of the country differently. They modernized northern Sudan, where most of the people lived, expanding telegraph and rail services and helping farmers grow cotton and other cash crops for export. At the same time, believing that the south was not ready for modernization, the British issued laws that prohibited outsiders from working or traveling there. The British discouraged the black African tribesmen from adopting Islam, speaking

Britain's long rule in Sudan (1899–1956) is evident in this photograph of Khartoum, taken around 1936. The statue depicts Herbert Horatio Kitchener, the British general who defeated the Sudanese army at the Battle of Omdurman in 1898.

Arabic, or dressing like their northern countrymen. Instead they encouraged the spread of Christianity and allowed Christian missionaries to enter the area and establish churches and schools. The British also permitted greater tribal autonomy in the south than in the north.

Although Sudan was generally peaceful during the condominium period, the region had its problems. After the end of World War I (1914–18), the Ottoman Empire was dissolved and its former Arab territories in the Middle East and Africa were divided among European countries like France and Great Britain. However, many Arabs wanted complete freedom from foreign control, and independence movements grew. In Sudan, groups like the White Flag League and the Umma Party urged freedom from Britain and Egypt during the 1920s and 1930s.

World War II (1939–1945) interrupted the debate on Sudanese independence, but by the late 1940s the issue emerged again. In 1948 the pro-independence Umma Party gained control of Sudan's legislative council and negotiated greater freedoms from British control. In February 1953, Egypt and Great Britain signed an agreement establishing a three-year transition period. Sudan would become independent on January 1, 1956.

CIVIL WAR BEGINS IN SUDAN

Sectional trouble started even before independence. Some Sudanese from the south, afraid Muslim Arabs would dominate the country, began waging a guerrilla war in the fall of 1955. They wanted to southern Sudan to become a separate country. This conflict, known as the First Sudanese Civil War, would continue on and off for the next 17 years.

The civilian government elected in 1956 was soon overthrown by a military *coup* led by two generals, Ibrahim Abbud and Ahmad Abd al Wahab. By 1959, Abbud had complete control of Sudan's government. His policies toward southern Sudan fueled the growing insurgency there. Abbud's government tried to suppress the culture and religious beliefs of people in the south by imposing those of the Arab and Islamic north.

In addition to the civil war, the Abbud government faced opposition from other groups, including the Sudanese Communist Party and the United National Front. After riots by students, civil servants, and trade unionists in October 1964, Abbud dissolved the military regime and reinstituted a civilian government. The new government would operate under the transitional constitution of the 1950s. Sirr al-Khatim al-Khalifa was named prime minister, and a 15-seat parliament was chosen and charged with writing a new constitution for Sudan.

Elections were held in March 1965, but continuing unrest in the south prevented many people from voting. The newly elected government, led by Muhammad Ahmad Mahjub, cracked down on communists and the southern guerrillas. However, the government remained unstable. Disagreements over Sudan's direction forced Mahjub to resign as prime minister in July 1966. He was succeeded by Sadiq al-Mahdi, the son of the country's Islamic religious leader. When al-Mahdi's government also lost public confidence, Mahjub returned to power as prime minister. In 1969, a military dictator named Jaafar al-Nimeri seized control of the government.

Throughout the 1960s, the civil war drained the country of resources. By 1972, about 500,000 people had been killed in southern Sudan—80 percent of them civilians. Hoping to end the fighting and reunify the country, Nimeri agreed to negotiate with Joseph Lagu, the leader of the Southern Sudan Liberation Movement (SSLM), the main opposition group. After a conference at Addis Ababa, Ethiopia, the two sides reached an agreement. The Addis Ababa accords, signed in March 1972, provided for a cease-fire and gave the southern region some autonomy.

A SHORT-LIVED PEACE

The Addis Ababa accords brought a decade of relative peace to Sudan. However, during this time the popularity of Nimeri's government declined because of its corruption and incompetence. A drought and subsequent famine, as well as a weak economy, did not help matters. To gain support, Nimeri aligned with a *fundamentalist* Muslim party called the National Islamic Front (NIF). In 1983, he declared that all of Sudan would be subject to Islamic law (known as *Sharia*). Many people in the south were unwilling to accept this, and war erupted again. The conflict between the Sudanese People's Liberation Movement (SPLM) soon turned into a full-scale civil war. The SPLM's military arm, the Sudanese People's Liberation Army (SPLA), soon took control of many rural communities in southern Sudan.

Jaafar al-Nimeri's decision to impose Islamic law on Sudan in 1983 caused leaders in southern Sudan to restart a civil war.

Because of Sudan's many problems, Nimeri's government was overthrown by the military in 1985. A transition-

Hassan al-Turabi engineered the 1989 coup that brought General Omar al-Bashir to power. However, the onetime allies became political enemies after Turabi was elected speaker of Sudan's assembly in 1996. On Bashir's orders, Turabi has been arrested many times.

al government, led by Lieutenant General Abd ar Rahman Siwar adh Dhahab, was created. Siwar adh Dhahab wanted Sudan to have a democratic government and called for free elections in 1986. When the people went to the polls they returned former prime minister Sadiq al-Mahdi to power.

The Mahdi government was unable to end the civil war or solve the country's economic problems. Hoping for a breakthrough, Sadiq al-Mahdi promised to withdraw *Sharia* as the law of Sudan in 1989. However, on the day the law was to be changed, his government was overthrown by *Islamists*. The coup was planned by Hassan al-Turabi, the leader of the National Islamic Front, and carried out by General Omar Hassan al-Bashir, who became president.

Bashir declared *martial law*. He banned political parties and labor unions and reinstituted harsh *Sharia* punishments. By 1990 the National Congress Party, a political arm of the National Islamic Front, had gained significant power in Sudan's parliament. In 1990–91, Turabi formed an organization for militants, the Popular Arab Islamic Conference (PAIC), which was based in Khartoum. This group opposed the 1991 Gulf War against Iraq, and allowed anti-western Islamists to operate freely in

Sudan. The most notorious example is Osama bin Laden, who trained terrorists in Sudan until 1996, when the U.S. pressured the Sudanese government to expel him.

In August 1998, Islamic demonstrators attacked the U.S. embassies in Kenya and Tanzania, killing 12 Americans and 300 Africans. In response, the U.S. fired cruise missiles at the al-Shifa pharmaceutical factory in Khartoum. The CIA believed that the plant was secretly being used to manufacture nerve gas and was linked to bin Laden's terrorist organization al-Qaeda. (This claim has never been proven or disproven.)

John Garang led the Sudan People's Liberation Army during the Second Sudanese Civil War (1983-2005).

A BREAK IN THE FIGHTING

Efforts to end Sudan's civil war continued through the 1990s. By 2002, the U.S. Committee for Refugees reported that more than 2 million Sudanese had died from fighting, disease, or famine since the second civil war began. Some 4 million Sudanese were displaced from their homes by the conflict, with at least 500,000 living as refugees in other countries.

In October 2002, the Sudanese government and SPLA rebels agreed to a cease-fire while representatives of the two sides met in Kenya to discuss a peaceful settlement. Peace talks continued through 2003 and 2004. On January 9, 2005, representatives of both sides signed the Naivasha Treaty.

This agreement called for southern autonomy for six years. At the end of that period, the people of the South would vote to either become independent, or to remain part of Sudan. The agreement also stipulated that all revenue from the state—particularly money from the sale of Sudan's oil and natural gas— would be shared between the northern and southern regions.

Although the treaty officially ended the civil war after 21 years, there were incidents of fighting on both sides between 2005 and the 2011 referendum. However, the focus of the international community turned to the Sudan government's involvement in another internal war—the Darfur conflict in western Sudan.

Leaders of Sudan's warring factions join hands in a symbolic gesture of unity as a new government is installed in 2005. Pictured are (left to right) John Garang, who became the vice president of Sudan in the new government; President Omar Al-Bashir; and Second Vice President Ali Osman Mohamed Taha.

CONFLICT IN DARFUR

The Darfur conflict began as a rivalry between farmers and herdsmen over pastureland. The farmers, many of whom were of African descent, attempted to prevent nomadic herdsmen of Arab ethnicity, known as the Baggara, from grazing their flocks on land used for their crops. The Baggara responded by attacking villages and forcing out the farmers.

In 2003 two groups, the Justice and Equality Movement (JEM) and the Sudanese Liberation Army, rebelled against the government, claiming that it had sided with the Baggara by assisting an Arab militia called the *janjaweed*. Both sides have been accused of significant human rights violations, including looting, rapes, mass killings, and the destruction of entire villages. In particular, the *janjaweed* has been accused of carrying out a policy of "ethnic cleansing" in the Darfur region.

The African Union brokered a ceasefire in April 2004 and sent peacekeeping troops in to ensure compliance. However, the conflict continued, and by 2006 the United Nations estimated that over 400,000 people had been killed in Darfur, with another 2 million people driven from their homes. That year the UN proposed sending a larger peacekeeping force of more than 17,000 soldiers to replace the smaller African Union force. However, Sudan refused to allow the UN peacekeepers into the country. Instead, the government launched a major military offensive against the rebel groups.

Unlike Sudan's first and second civil wars, religion does not play an important part in the fighting, as most of the combatants on all sides are Muslims. Additionally, in recent years some groups of Darfuri Arabs have

The conflict in Darfur drew international attention. This photo was taken at a "Save Darfur" rally in Washington, D.C.

begun waging their own armed rebellion against the Arab government and its *janjaweed* allies, which they say do not represent them.

During the years of fighting, there have been several cease-fire agreements in hopes of negotiating a peace, but none have lasted. The most recent came in February 2010, when the Justice and Equality Movement agreed to talks with the Sudanese government. However, the peace was broken when JEM accused the government of bombing a village, and said it would no longer negotiate with the regime.

SECESSION OF SOUTH SUDAN, AND WAR

In January 2011, the long-planned referendum required by the Naivasha Agreement on the status of South Sudan was held. When the votes were counted, more than 90 percent of the residents of South Sudan had voted for independence, rather than to remain part of Sudan. The date for South Sudan to gain its independence was set for July 9, 2011.

The referendum vote did not go smoothly in all areas. The government did not permit voting in the Abyei region, where many Dinka live. This area is on the border between northern and southern Sudan, and contains valuable oil fields. The native people of Abyei were expected to vote to join South Sudan. Today, both countries claim the disputed area, although it is currently occupied by Sudanese troops.

The independence of South Sudan was supposed to mark the start of a new period of peaceful cooperation. However, in less than a year unresolved issues like the status of Sudan's Abyei oil fields brought the neighboring countries to war again.

In the spring of 2012 fighting flared up over the oilfields in Abyei, with Sudan launching air strikes into South Sudan. Both the African Union and the United Nations immediately stepped in to try to avert war. However, with both sides beginning to dig in for a long fight, it was clear to international observers that South Sudan's independence alone would not end the fighting that has plagued this region for decades.

Sudan remains dominated by its authoritarian president, Omar al-Bashir (opposite), who is pictured addressing the United Nations. (Right) Ballots from the January 2011 referendum are sorted and counted in the presence of election observers at a polling centre in Aweil, southern Sudan.

3 Politics in Sudan and South Sudan

FOLLOWING THE JANUARY 2011 REFERENDUM, South Sudan seceded from Sudan in July 2011, creating two countries. Sudan and South Sudan have separate political systems that are different in many ways. However, they also have many similarities, in part due to the shared history of the two countries.

THE GOVERNMENT OF SUDAN

Sudan's constitution, which was adopted in 1998, gives most political power to the president. As head of government and chief of state, the president commands the military, appoints judges, and rules over a cabinet that oversees various departments of government. The president has the power to make laws and can even amend the constitution.

Sudan's current president, Omar al-Bashir, headed a military *junta* that took power in 1989. At the time his government had strong support from the National Congress Party (NCP), the political arm of the National Islamic Front (NIF). However, Bashir gradually moved to expand his power, and in December 1999 he dissolved Sudan's parliament over a split with NIF leader Hassan al-Turabi, the speaker of parliament and his former ally. Turabi had attempted to amend Sudan's constitution to limit the president's authority. In response Bashir took measures to preserve his rule and restrict Turabi's influence, imprisoning his rival several times.

The presidency is an elective office, and presidents are supposed to serve five-year terms. In the most recent election, held in 2010, Bashir received more than 68 percent of the vote. However, although opposition parties participated, most observers noted that they are only allowed because they have no real chance of gaining power.

Under the terms of the 2005 peace agreement, two vice presidents were chosen to serve under the president—one from the north and one from the south. Initially, SPLM leader John Garang was the vice president representing the south; however, after his death in a plane crash in July 2005, his deputy Salva Kiir Mayardit filled the position. Kiir held this position until July 2011, when he became the first president of South Sudan. In September 2011, the former Second Vice President Ali Osman Taha took over Kiir's position as First Vice President, and Adam Yousef, a representative from Darfur, was appointed Second Vice President.

The president is also served by a group of ministers, each of whom oversees a government department such as agriculture, defense, energy, mining, and education. The power of ministers is limited, as the president has the authority to remove them at any time.

As part of the 2005 power-sharing agreement, a new parliament was created in Sudan. The National Legislature has two chambers: the National Assembly (Majlis Watani) and the Council of States (Majlis Welayat). All members of the legislature serve six-year terms.

The National Assembly includes 450 members who are appointed by the president. The functions of the National Assembly include monitoring the performance of the president and ministers; passing bills and laws; ratifying international treaties; and approving the annual budget.

The Council of States includes 50 members elected by the legislatures of Sudan's states. The Council is responsible for overseeing relations between the states and the federal government. In addition, presidential appointments to the Constitutional Court must be approved by two-thirds of the members of the Council of States.

The president, ministers, and members of the National Legislature can all propose new laws. These are introduced into one chamber of the National Legislature, where they are reviewed and voted upon. If the law passes in one chamber, the other chamber must also pass the law before it can go into effect.

At the top of Sudan's judicial system is a Supreme Court, which is headed by a chief justice. The Supreme Court, or Court of Cassation, is the highest level court; appeals cannot be taken any higher. However, the Supreme Court does not oversee cases concerning the constitutionality of law. Instead, a Constitutional Court performs *judicial review*—determining whether a new law conflicts with the constitution—and hears cases concerning citizens' constitutional rights. The president appoints members of this court, but the appointments must be confirmed by the Council of States.

There are four levels of criminal and civil courts. These include Town Benches, where local matters are resolved; District Courts; Province Courts; and the Court of Appeals. This court examines cases to make sure that lower court rulings were fair and in compliance with Sudanese law.

The 2005 constitution of Sudan adopted the Islamic legal code *Sharia* as the basis for national laws, while allowing for a non-*Sharia* code in the southern states. Since the 2011 division of Sudan and South Sudan, some Islamist leaders have pressured President Bashir to replace the 2005 constitution with a new document that follows the *Sharia* code even more strictly. In 2012, a coalition of groups called the Islamic Constitution Front (ICF) proposed the Draft Constitution of Sudan, which was based entirely on *Sharia* law.

THE GOVERNMENT OF SOUTH SUDAN

In 2005, the Southern Sudan Legislative Assembly was established. This body made decisions on internal affairs of southern Sudan during the six-year period it was still part of Sudan. After the 2011 referendum vote, the Legislative Assembly produced and ratified a constitution for the Republic of South Sudan. This constitution was signed by the new president, Salva Kiir , during the independence day ceremony.

Following independence, the Southern Sudan Legislative Assembly was dissolved and a new legislature established. The National Legislature of South Sudan consists of two houses, the National Legislative Assembly and

Recruits for the Southern Sudan Police Service (SSPS) perform a training exercise at their academy in Rajaf, South Sudan.

the Council of States. These two bodies have functions similar to those of Sudan's National Legislature. Representatives are to be elected for four-year terms, beginning from July 9, 2011.

The government of South Sudan is currently led by President Salva Kiir and Vice President Riek Machar. The president has significant powers in South Sudan. These include the authority to relieve an elected state governor or to dissolve a state legislative assembly. The president can also declare war or a state of emergency without requiring the approval of the National Legislature.

Riek Machar serves as vice president of South Sudan.

About 80 percent of Sudan's people work in agriculture. (Opposite) A herdsman leads goats to drink in a nearby river. (Right) Farmers harvest peanuts, one of Sudan's main export crops.

4 Struggling Economies

Both Sudan and South Sudan are poor countries with few paved roads, inadequate supplies of clean water, shortages of skilled labor, and relatively little arable land. Add to the mix sectional conflicts, frequent droughts, and high *inflation* and it is easy to understand why both countries rank low on measures of economic productivity.

Before the secession of South Sudan, Sudan's *gross domestic product* (GDP), a measure of the market value of all goods and services produced in the country annually, was about $97 billion, according to the World Bank. However, that economic measure has fallen since the July 2011 secession, since South Sudan contains most of the country's oil fields. Oil had driven much of Sudan's growth in GDP since the country began exporting oil in 1999. Without oil, Sudan has struggled to maintain economic stability.

Even without the disputed Abyei oil fields, after secession South Sudan ended up with about 75 percent of Sudan's oil fields. In the formerly united Sudanese state, oil had been transported from the fields in the south through a pipeline north to Port Sudan, where it could be loaded onto supertankers for export to other countries. However, in January 2012 South Sudan shut down oil production because it claimed that the fees Sudan wanted to charge to use the pipeline were too high. This disagreement—which cost the government of Sudan billions in fees and oil export revenue—was a key reason for the border conflict over the oil fields that erupted in the spring of 2012.

THE ECONOMY OF SUDAN

From 1999 until 2008, the economy of Sudan grew thanks to high global oil prices and significant inflows of foreign investment in Sudanese companies. With revenue from oil sharply curtailed, the government has attempted to generate new sources of revenues, such as from gold mining, while carrying out an austerity program to reduce expenditures.

Eighty percent of Sudanese workers make their livings farming. Cotton, peanuts, sesame seeds, and grains like sorghum, *millet*, and wheat are grown—both for use in the country and for export. Agriculture contributes about 45 percent of Sudan's GDP.

Sudan is the world's second-largest producer of gum arabic, a product of the acacia tree. The resin can be used to replace oil in low-fat baked goods, to thicken candies, in the adhesive on postage stamps, and to stabilize the foam in beer and soda. Before the civil war, Sudan had been the world's top producer of gum arabic but now it shares the market with the neighboring

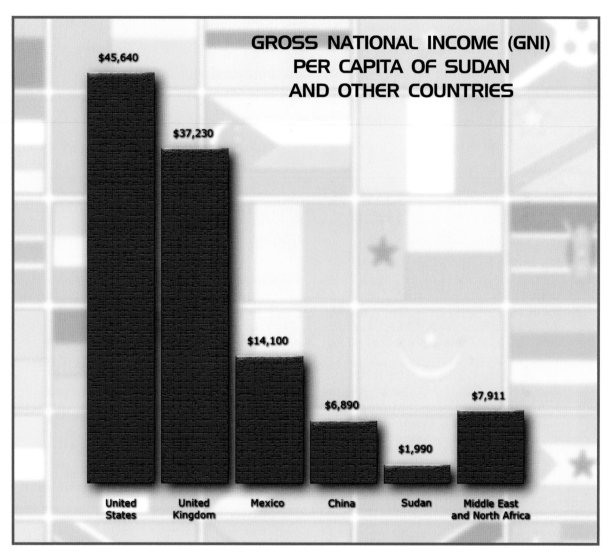

GROSS NATIONAL INCOME (GNI) PER CAPITA OF SUDAN AND OTHER COUNTRIES

- $45,640 — United States
- $37,230 — United Kingdom
- $14,100 — Mexico
- $6,890 — China
- $1,990 — Sudan
- $7,911 — Middle East and North Africa

Gross national income per capita is the total value of all goods and services produced domestically in a year, supplemented by income received from abroad, divided by midyear population. The above figures take into account fluctuations in currency exchange rates and differences in inflation rates across global economies, so that an international dollar has the same purchasing power as a U.S. dollar has in the United States. Source: World Bank, 2011.

country of Chad. Chad began processing the resin at the urging of food and cosmetic industry users, who feared instability in Sudan would prevent them from obtaining this key ingredient in their products.

Industrial development in Sudan is relatively limited. This aspect of the country's economy is dominated by the processing of agricultural products, such as sugar and cotton. Cement, soap, shoe manufacturing, petroleum

THE ECONOMY OF SUDAN

Gross domestic product (GDP*): $97.21 billion

Inflation: 9%

Natural resources: petroleum; small reserves of iron ore, copper, chromium ore, zinc, tungsten, mica, silver, gold, hydropower

Agriculture (44.7% of GDP): cotton, groundnuts (peanuts), sorghum, millet, wheat, gum arabic, sugarcane, cassava (tapioca), mangoes, papaya, bananas, sweet potatoes, sesame; sheep and other livestock

Industry (45% of GDP): oil, cotton ginning, textiles, cement, edible oils, sugar, soap distilling, shoes, petroleum refining, pharmaceuticals, armaments, automobile/light truck assembly

Services (10.3% of GDP): government services, other

Foreign trade:
Exports–$7.705 billion: oil and petroleum products; cotton, sesame, livestock, groundnuts, gum arabic, sugar.
Imports–$8.427 billion: foodstuffs, manufactured goods, refinery and transport equipment, medicines and chemicals, textiles, wheat.

Economic growth rate: -0.2%

Currency exchange rate: U.S. $1 = 2.68 Sudanese pounds (2012)

*GDP is the total value of goods and services produced in a country annually.
All figures are 2011 estimates unless otherwise indicated.
Source: CIA World Factbook, 2012.

refining, and the manufacture of armaments and automobiles round out the list of the country's biggest industries. Much of Sudan's industry is located in or near the city of Khartoum North (Bahri). In recent years, the Giad Industrial Complex in Al Jazirah state introduced the assembly of small autos and trucks, as well as some military equipment. The government of Sudan owns some of the industrial plants, while others are privately owned. Industry employs about 7 percent of Sudan's workforce, and contributes about 45 percent to Sudan's GDP.

In 2011 Sudan introduced a new currency, still called the Sudanese pound, but the value of the currency has fallen since its introduction and shortages of foreign exchange continue. Sudan also faces rising inflation—a rate of about 16 percent in 2011—which led to several protests in Khartoum during early 2012.

Sudan's involvement in the border war with South Sudan, as well as the ongoing Darfur conflict, along with its lack of basic infrastructure in large areas, high rate of unemployment, and reliance by much of the population on subsistence agriculture ensure that most of Sudan's people will remain at or below the poverty line for years to come.

THE ECONOMY OF SOUTH SUDAN

Due to decades of civil war with the north, industry and infrastructure in South Sudan are severely underdeveloped. South Sudan has just 37 miles (60 km) of paved roads. Electricity is produced mostly by costly diesel generators. Poverty is widespread, as most of the people in this country make their living through subsistence farming, growing enough to feed their families.

New construction in Juba, the capital of South Sudan. Historically, the capital was largely composed of primitive slum areas, but since South Sudan became independent its has seen new investment in facilities and infrastructure..

Despite these problems, South Sudan does have several economic advantages over Sudan that could be exploited for economic growth. First is its control over the oil fields, as South Sudan can produce approximately 375,000 barrels of this valuable resource per day. However, until the 2012 pipeline dispute is resolved, the landlocked country will be unable to bring its oil to the market. It will take years and billions of dollars for South Sudan to construct a new pipeline to reach another port, so it makes economic sense for South Sudan to work out a reasonable fee with Sudan to use the existing pipeline to Port Sudan.

Another advantage for South Sudan is that the White Nile valley is one of the richest agricultural areas in Africa. It has fertile soils and an abundant supply of water. Currently the region supports approximately 15 million head of cattle. The White Nile also has a sufficiently strong flow to generate large quantities of hydroelectricity, but this will require significant investment to achieve.

Decades of fighting and lack of infrastructure have prevented South Sudan from developing a tourist industry. However, the country is home to large herds of wildlife, which could be exploited in the future to attract tourists.

South Sudan does not have significant debt, because Sudan maintained responsibility for its debt when South Sudan seceded. In addition, the country has received billions of dollars in foreign aid, primarily from the United States, Great Britain, Norway, and the Netherlands. The World Bank has announced that it will provide funds to build South Sudan's infrastructure, improve its agricultural output, and increase power generation. However, the economy of South Sudan will probably remain linked to Sudan for many years.

Many cultural and ethnic groups live in Sudan. (Opposite) A woman and her children walk from the bazaar in Khartoum, Sudan. (Right) A young girl of the nomadic Ngok Dinka tribe of the Sudan leads cattle to water and food in the Abyei region that is disputed by Sudan and South Sudan. The Dinka are South Sudan's largest ethnic group, numbering about 1.5 million.

5 The People of Sudan and South Sudan

Before South Sudan gained its independence in 2011, the country of Sudan was home to more than 40 million people from many different ethnic and religious backgrounds. These differences contributed to the decades of fighting within the country.

From 1956 until 2011, Sudan's major cities and much of its industry were concentrated in the north, where the culture is predominantly Muslim and dominated by Arabs. Modern automobiles and other conveniences were common in the cities. In southern Sudan, the culture was more traditionally African. The division of the country into Sudan and South Sudan in 2011 reinforced those differences.

EVERYDAY LIFE IN SUDAN

Today the population of Sudan is estimated at about 34 million. About 70 percent of the population are Sudanese Arabs. The rest are members of African tribes like the Fur, Beja, Nuba, and Fallata. The Fur primarily live in the western Sudan province of Darfur, where they are the largest tribe. The Beja are a group of nomadic camel and goat herders who have been living in Eastern Sudan for 4,000 years.

The Nuba are people who live in the Nuba Mountains of Sudan's South Kordofan province. Unlike most of the rest of the people of Sudan, the Nuba

THE PEOPLE OF SUDAN

Population: 34,206,710 (July 2012 est.)

Ethnic groups: Sudanese Arab (approximately 70%), Fur, Beja, Nuba, Fallata

Languages: Arabic (official), English (official), Nubian, Ta Bedawie, Fur

Age structure:
  0–14 years: 42.1%
  15–64 years: 55.2%
  65 years and over: 2.7%

Birth rate: 31.7 births/1,000 population

Infant mortality rate: 55.63 deaths/1,000 live births

Death rate: 8.33 deaths/1,000 population

Population growth rate: 1.88%

Life expectancy at birth:
  total population: 62.57 years
  male: 60.58 years
  female: 64.67 years

Total fertility rate: 4.17 children born/woman

Religions: Sunni Muslim (97%), small Christian minority

Literacy: 61.1% (2003 est.)

All figures are 2012 estimates unless otherwise indicated.
Source: Adapted from CIA World Factbook, 2012.

Most of these Sudanese Muslims are wearing traditional gowns (*jalabiyyas*) and white turbans (*emmas*).

have historically sided with the southern Sudanese against Sudan's government. However, in the 2011 referendum the Nuba of South Kordofan were not permitted to participate in the secession of South Sudan.

Most citizens of Sudan speak Arabic as well as a native language (for example, Nubian, Beja, Fur, Nuba, or Ingessana). In the cities, many people also speak English, which is the country's official language.

Nearly all of Sudan's people follow Islam, a religion first preached by the Prophet Muhammad during the early seventh century. All Muslims are expected to observe five important precepts, also known as the Pillars of Islam. The most important of these is the belief in a single god (Allah) and that Muhammad was his prophet. Each Muslim is also required to pray at different times during each day; give charitable donations to the needy; observe ritual fasting during the holy month of Ramadan; and visit the holy city of Mecca in Saudi Arabia at least once during his or her lifetime, if physically and financially able to do so.

Sharia is a code of behavior based on Islamic scriptures and traditions; it spells out the moral goals of the community and is the basis of laws in some Muslim countries. In Sudan, courts look to this religious *Sharia* law for guidance when interpreting the law and enforcing justice.

Although some Sudanese, particularly professionals, may wear business dress or western attire, traditionally Muslims living in the country wear long gowns called *jalabiyyas*. They cover their heads in either white or orange skull caps or white turbans called *emmas*. Women traditionally wear a colorful fabric garment, called a *tobe*, which is ten yards long; they wrap these *tobes* around their heads and bodies, obscuring the dresses they wear underneath.

EVERYDAY LIFE IN SOUTH SUDAN

South Sudan has a population of around 10.6 million. Its people are members of approximately 60 different tribal or ethnic groups. The major ethnic groups in South Sudan are the Dinka, at more than 1.5 million, the Nuer (about 1 million), the Nuba, the Bari, and the Azande. The Shilluk constitute a historically influential state along the White Nile, and their language is closely related to Dinka and Nuer. The traditional territories of the Shilluk and the Northeastern Dinka are adjacent.

Many of the people living in southern Sudan are farmers and herders.

Among the Dinka and other nomadic tribes, cows are considered much more than farm animals; they represent wealth and prestige. During the rainy season (April to October), the Dinka live in villages of small homes built from mud and grass, where they cultivate the grain millet. During the dry season, those Dinka who are healthy take their herds to camps by the river.

Because of the diversity of tribes, over 60 indigenous languages are spoken in South Sudan. The indigenous languages with the most speakers are Dinka, Nuer, Bari, and Zande. In South Sudan's capital city, an Arabic pidgin known as Juba Arabic is used by several thousand people. English is the country's official language.

THE PEOPLE OF SOUTH SUDAN

Population: 10,625,176 (July 2012 est.)
Ethnic groups: Dinka, Kakwa, Bari, Azande, Shilluk, Kuku, Murle, Mandari, Didinga, Ndogo, Bviri, Lndi, Anuak, Bongo, Lango, Dungotona, Acholi
Age structure:
  0–14 years: 44.4%
  15–64 years: 53%
  65 years and over: 2.6%
Infant mortality rate: 71.83 deaths/1,000 live births

Population growth rate: 2.55%
Religions: animist, Christian
Languages: English (official), Arabic (includes Juba and Sudanese variants) (official), regional languages include Dinka, Nuer, Bari, Zande, Shilluk
Literacy: 27%

All figures are 2012 estimates unless otherwise indicated.
Source: Adapted from CIA World Factbook, 2012.

A Dinka village in South Sudan.

Many of the people of South Sudan practice traditional African religions. Most African traditional religions are based on the belief that spirits exist in everything in nature—people, animals, plants, and even stones. To win the favor of spirits, religious rituals, including the sacrifice of oxen, are sometimes performed. The spirits of ancestors are also believed to affect the daily lives of tribe members.

It is believed that approximately half of the people of South Sudan practice Christianity. This religion has a long history in Sudan, dating back nearly 2,000 years. Since the 1980s, Christian missionaries have been more active in southern Sudan.

South Sudan is much more rural than Sudan, with many people making their living through subsistence farming. The constant warfare has resulted in a lack of infrastructure such as roads, electricity, and communications facilities in the region.

EDUCATION IN SUDAN AND SOUTH SUDAN

Primary and secondary education in both Sudan and South Sudan are free, although there are few schools in the south and not enough teachers. As a result, few children living in the southern part of the country attend school. Less than 30 percent of the population of South Sudan is able to read and write. Girls are much less likely to get an education in Sudan than their broth-

Fur children at school in Arabashir village near El Fasher, North Darfur.

ers. The literacy rate in Sudan is more than twice as high, at 61 percent.

Overall, few students graduate from high school in Sudan or South Sudan, but those who do graduate may attend one of Sudan's public universities. The oldest and largest of these is the government-run University of Khartoum. With campuses in Khartoum, Khartoum North, and Omdurman, the university has about 17,000 undergraduate and 6,000 postgraduate students enrolled. However, students cannot attend the university unless they join the Popular Defense Forces, a paramilitary group associated with the National Congress Party. Once enrolled they may pursue degrees in both *Sharia* and English law as well as agriculture and veterinary sciences, engineering, computer sciences, pharmacy, nursing, architecture, management, and medicine.

Other schools in Sudan include Ahfad University College for Women in Omdurman, the leading women's college in Sudan, and Omdurman Ahlia University, a private school that opened in 1982.

There are six public universities in South Sudan, including the University of Juba, the University of Bahr El-Ghazal in Wau, the University of Northern Bahr El-Ghazal in Aweil, Upper Nile University in Malakal, and Rumbek University.

HEALTH CARE IN SUDAN AND SOUTH SUDAN

Physicians are in short supply in both Sudan and South Sudan, and in both countries doctors must contend with drug shortages and poorly equipped medical facilities. In Sudan there is one doctor for every 6,500 people in the north; the ratio is even worse—one doctor for every 83,000 people—in South

Sudan. Doctors must treat people for diseases rarely found in the developed world—tuberculosis, malaria, snail fever, dysentery, sleeping sickness, black fever, and measles.

The infant mortality rate, which measures the percentage of children who die under one year of age, is one way of assessing the health care system of a country. Both Sudan and South Sudan score very poorly when compared to other countries around the

A doctor examines children at a medical clinic in Nyala, Sudan, run by the United Nations.

world. Sudan's 2012 infant mortality rate of 55.63 deaths to 1,000 live births ranks 184th out of 220 countries. South Sudan's 2012 rate, 71.83 deaths per 1,000 live births, is even worse, ranking 201st out of 220 countries.

Until recently the government of Sudan denied that the virus HIV, which causes the disease AIDS, was a problem in the country. AIDS destroys a person's immune system, making him or her fatally susceptible to normally non-threatening diseases. However, recent reports by UNAIDS, an organization that tracks the spread of the disease throughout the world, indicate that about 1.1 percent of Sudan's population, and more than 3 percent of South Sudan's population, are infected with HIV or AIDS.

(Opposite) Aerial view of Khartoum, Sudan's largest city, with the Nile River flowing past the city in the background. (Right) Aircraft on the runway at Juba Airport, which serves the capital city of South Sudan. With a population of about 250,000, Juba is much smaller than Khartoum and many other cities in Sudan.

6 Sudanese Communities

When South Sudan seceded from Sudan in July 2011, all of the most populous cities (those with more than half a million people) were located in the northern part of the country. The largest city in South Sudan is Juba, the capital, with an estimated population of about 250,000. Khartoum, Khartoum North (Bahri), and Omdurman make up Sudan's biggest metropolis, together housing an estimated 6.3 million people. Port Sudan, home to about 500,000 people, is indispensable to Sudan's economy as it is the only seaport.

KHARTOUM AND BAHRI

The best-known city in Sudan is Khartoum, which in Arabic means "elephant trunk," a shape the city resembles from above. The city is located at the spot where the Blue Nile and White Nile come together. It is connected to its nearby

The Al-Mogran Mosque in Khartoum is located at the point where the Blue Nile and White Nile meet.

sister cities of Bahri (also known as Khartoum North) and Omdurman by bridges. As the capital of Sudan, Khartoum is home to embassies and other government-related offices. Most of the country's businesses are headquartered there, along with many of the country's doctors and professionals.

Despite being the country's capital, Khartoum is not a big tourist destination. It has only 11 hotels. Only recently has the city's telephone system become reliable. There is one television station in the entire country and few radio stations. From midnight to 5 A.M. in Khartoum, people on the streets are subject to questioning by the police. Foreigners may be asked to show their passports. Furthermore, no photographs can be taken within the city without a permit, and photographs of military areas, bridges, public utilities, broadcasting stations, and street people are never allowed.

Visitors to Khartoum North will find dockyards, meat packing plants, textile weaving enterprises, rubber plants, concrete manufacturing, and shoe manufacturing. Khartoum North also contains some of the most expensive houses in the area. In nearby Omdurman, mud-walled houses are typical abodes for city workers.

A sad legacy of Sudan's civil war can be seen on the streets of Khartoum, where thousands of homeless orphans must fend for themselves. More than a million Sudanese still live in refugee camps near the city.

OMDURMAN

About 2.4 million people live in Omdurman, a city that is not quite as modern as Khartoum. Roads in Omdurman are unpaved, and there is no commercial center. However, the city does have the largest marketplace in Sudan, the Souk el-Kebir. For 1,800 years peddlers and craftsman have lined its narrow streets, jostling for customers. At the *souk* one can purchase food, handmade crafts and jewelry, and many other items. Located near the *souk* is a more specialized marketplace—Omdurman's camel market (the Mowelih).

Omdurman is also home to the Mahdi's tomb and to the Khalifa's House Museum. The original Mahdi's tomb was destroyed when the British recaptured the city, but because of the tomb's historical significance it was rebuilt in 1947.

Omdurman is famous for its *dervishes*, religious Muslims who dance themselves into a frenzy every Friday. Dressed in white from their turbans to their jalabiyyas, these men gather in western Omdurman in front of the tomb of Sheikh Hamad al-Nile, a 19th century holy man who was believed to be able to perform miracles. The dervishes form a circle and, to the beat of drums and chants, whirl around in dizzying fashion to remove themselves from everyday life and become closer to God.

PORT SUDAN

Port Sudan, the country's only seaport, is located on the Red Sea about 800 miles (1,287 km) northeast of Khartoum. It is through Port Sudan that the Sudanese trade their goods with the rest of the world. The British established the city in 1905; today it is home to about a million people, including refugees from Chad, Uganda, Eritrea, and Ethiopia. Pilgrims on the way to Mecca in Saudi Arabia often pass through the city.

While Port Sudan is not the thriving terminal it once was, there are signs that its fortunes may be improving. An international chain recently built a luxury hotel in the city. Also encouraging was the news that Ethiopia, which has no seaport of its own, has agreed to use Port Sudan for its shipping needs. Most importantly, a pipeline completed in 1999 is capable of carrying oil from the fields in Sudan and South Sudan to tankers anchored at the port.

JUBA

Juba is the capital of Southern Sudan, as well as of the Sudanese state of Central Equatoria. It is located on the White Nile River and is an important river port. Although Juba is the largest city in the region, it is primarily made up of mud huts and derelict buildings. Electrical service and clean water are often unavailable to the city's residents.

Juba was once a transportation center, with highways to neighboring countries like Kenya, Uganda, and the Democratic Republic of the Congo. However, during the Second Sudanese Civil War a great deal of fighting occurred around the city and the road network was essentially destroyed. The roads are only now being repaired.

Juba is a sprawling community surrounded by slums like this one.

A CALENDAR OF SUDANESE FESTIVALS

Muslim Holidays

The dates of Muslim holidays, such as **Ramadan**, are determined using a lunar calendar that is shorter than the 365-day solar year used in Western countries. This means that each year, Muslim holidays are held 10 or 11 days earlier than the year before. Thus, any Muslim holiday could be celebrated during any month in the Western calendar.

The **Muslim New Year** marks the beginning of the Islamic month known as Muharram.

Mawlid an-Nabi, the commemoration of the birthday of the Prophet Mohammed, is celebrated by prayer and often a procession to the local mosque. Families gather for feasts, often featuring the foods that were reportedly the favorites of Mohammed: dates, grapes, almonds, and honey. This holiday occurs on the 12th day of the month Rabi'-ul-Awwal.

The month of Ramadan is the holiest season of the year for Muslims. During Ramadan, Muslims are supposed to fast during the day, pray, and perform good deeds. At the end of Ramadan comes **Eid al-Fitr**, a feast and celebration lasting three days. This is a a joyous holiday in which Muslims visit family and friends, give gifts, and enjoy meals.

Eid al-Adha is celebrated on the 10th day of the Islamic month of Dhul Hijja. It observes the Prophet Abraham's willingness to sacrifice his son for God. It also marks the end of the *Hajj*, a ritual pilgrimage that all Muslims are expected to make to Mecca at least once during their lifetimes, if they are physically and financially able to do so.

January

Sudan has few national holidays. On January 1, the Sudanese people celebrate their liberation from the Egyptian and British Condominium Government on **Independence Day**. Soldiers parade through the streets of Khartoum to mark the occasion.

On January 7, members of the Coptic Christian Church celebrate **Christmas**, the birth of Jesus Christ. The Coptic Church is an ancient sect that once flourished in the region.

March

Unity Day, celebrated on March 27, commemorates the signing of the Addis Ababa agreement in 1972. The agreement ended the civil war for a time and gave hope that peace would last. It did not.

April

Christians celebrate the season of **Lent**, a time of prayer and self-sacrifice, between February and April; the dates of the season vary from year to year. Lent lasts for 40 days. The last week of Lent is known as Passion Week, and recognizes the arrival of Jesus in Jerusalem on **Palm Sunday**; the **Last Supper** on Holy Thursday; and the crucifixion on **Good Friday**. These are followed by **Easter Sunday**, when Christians celebrate the resurrection of Jesus. Easter always falls between March 22 and April 25.

June

Revolution Day, observed on June 30, commemorates the military coup that brought Omar al-Bashir to power in 1989.

July

South Sudan celebrates its **Independence Day** on July 9.

December

Christians who do not follow the Coptic tradition celebrate **Christmas** on December 25.

RECIPES

Maschi (Stuffed Tomato with Chopped Beef)

2 lbs. chopped beef
1 tsp. salt
1/2 tsp. pepper
1 tsp. garlic powder (or 2 cloves mashed)
4 tbs. chopped fresh dill (or 1 tsp. dried dill)
2 tbs. salad oil
1 cup cooked rice
8 large tomatoes
2 tbs. butter
2 tbs. oil

Sauce:
2 6 oz. cans tomato paste
2 6 oz. cans water
1/2 tsp. salt
1 tsp. cinnamon
1 tsp. garlic powder
green olives

Directions:
1. Sauté beef with salt, pepper, garlic powder, dill, and oil until meat browns. Add cooked rice.
2. Cut and open a slit in each tomato. Scoop out the inside of the tomato. Fill tomato with beef mixture and close slit.
3. Melt butter and oil in a skillet and sauté tomatoes until dark red. Remove tomatoes and place in a heavy saucepan.
4. Combine tomato paste, water, salt, cinnamon, and garlic powder and pour over tomatoes. Simmer over low heat for 10 to 15 minutes. Garnish with green olive slices.

Sudani Rice

3 cups rice
1 tbs. butter or oil
1 tsp. salt
pinch of turmeric (optional)
pinch of coriander (optional)
pinch of cardamom (optional)

Directions:
1. In pot, fry rice in butter or oil for 1 to 2 minutes. Pour water into pot until covering rice by an inch.
2. Add salt and turmeric or coriander or cardamom. Cover and cook until water evaporated.

Shorba

3 lbs. lamb bones
2 quarts water
2 tsp. salt
1/2 lb. whole onions, peeled
1/2 lb. carrots, peeled and cut in chunks
1/2 lb. cabbage, cut in small wedges
1/2 lb. string beans, trimmed
3 cloves garlic, chopped finely
4 tbs. peanut butter thinned with juice of 1 lemon

Directions:
1. Simmer lamb bones in water with salt for one hour. Add onions, carrots, cabbage, string beans, and garlic. Simmer for 1 hour until vegetables are thoroughly cooked.
2. Remove lamb bones and put the mixture through a sieve or food mill. Mix peanut butter with the juice of one lemon. Add peanut butter to soup puree. Season with salt and pepper.

GLOSSARY

condominium—a system under which a territory is ruled by two or more nations, which share equal rights to the land and resources. Such forms of rule are rare because they rely on the cooperation of multiple governments.

coup—the sudden overthrow of a government, especially by the military.

dervish—a follower of Sufism, or Islamic mysticism, whose style of worship includes using physical movement (such as dancing) to enter a trancelike state.

durra—a grain grown for food and animal feed in tropical or arid areas.

fundamentalist—someone who participates in a religious movement based on a literal interpretation of religious doctrine and strict adherence to that doctrine.

gross domestic product—the value of all goods and services produced in a country during a one-year period.

haboob—a violent dust storm that occurs in Sudan. These storms can blot out the sun, and people are advised to take shelter until they pass.

indigenous—native to a particular region.

inflation—an increase in the supply of money and credit relative to available goods and services, resulting in a continuing rise in the general price level.

Islamist—radical, militant, or extremist Muslim beliefs.

judicial review—the doctrine that gives courts the authority to determine whether laws are unconstitutional and have them nullified.

junta—a group that takes control of a country following a coup.

martial law—law administered by military forces during a period of war, unrest, or another emergency during which the civilian government may be unable to maintain order.

millet—a fast-growing cereal plant used for food in Africa.

savanna—a flat grassland in a tropical or subtropical region.

sorghum—a tall cereal grass cultivated in tropical areas as a grain crop and for animal feed.

steppe—an area of flat, treeless land similar to a prairie, but with short grasses.

talisman—an object that is believed to have magical powers or serve a religious purpose.

PROJECT AND REPORT IDEAS

Map the Conflict

Draw a map of Sudan and mark the individual states. Color the southern states a different color from the North. Include major topographical features like mountain ranges and the Nile River.

Study the Nile River

Draw a map which shows the Blue and White Nile rivers and where they meet. Research the sources of both rivers and explain how their water flows are different. How do these differences affect the Nile in Egypt?

Sides of the War

Civil war was a major component of Sudan's history. Research the culture of the North and the culture of the South. What do they believe? How are they different? How did the civil war start? How did it come to an end?

Learn through Cooking

Refer to the section on a traditional meal in Chapter 5 and the included recipes. Cook a dish and present it to the class. Explain how meals are served and how Islam influences what foods are eaten.

Ancient Sudan

At one time, the culture of Kush was much like that of Egypt. Research the kingdom of Kush and find out how they were similar to the Egyptians. Did they use hieroglyphics? Did they build pyramids?

Write a Biography

Chose a name from the following list of important figures from Sudan's history. Do research at the library or on the Internet to find out about this person, and write a one-page biography:

- Muhammad Ali
- Muhammad Ahmed (the Mahdi)
- Abdullah ibn Muhammad
- Charles Gordon
- Horatio Herbert Kitchener
- Ibrahim Abbud
- Sirr al-Khatim al-Khalifa
- Jaafar al-Nimeri
- Joseph Lagu
- Sadiq al-Mahdi
- Hassan al-Turabi
- Omar Hassan al-Bashir
- John Garang
- Salva Kiir Mayardit
- Riek Machar

CHRONOLOGY

ca. 2000 B.C.:	The early civilization of Kush trades with Egypt.
ca. 1500:	Kush becomes a province of Egypt under the rule of Pharaoh Ahmose I.
750:	The Kushite king Kashta conquers portions of Egypt.
ca. 600:	Merotic civilization begins to rise along the Nile.
24:	Angered by Merotic incursions into Roman-controlled Egypt, Roman legions invade Meroe and bring the region under imperial control.
ca. A.D. 570:	Muhammad, whose teaching will become the basis of Islam, is born; three Nubian kingdoms in the Sudan region (Nobatia, Muqurra, and Alwa) are converted to Christianity.
652:	Nubians resist the advance of Islam and sign a peace agreement.
1276:	The Mamluk rulers of Egypt gain power over Sudan.
1517:	The Ottoman Turks absorb Egypt and Sudan into their empire.
1820:	The Egyptian warlord Muhammad Ali sends a force to invade Sudan. The region soon comes under Egypt's control.
1869:	The Suez Canal opens.
1882:	Great Britain becomes involved in Egyptian and Sudanese affairs.
1883:	The Mahdi declares *jihad* against the foreign rule of the Sudan.
1898:	The forces of the *khalifa* are defeated by British troops under Lord Kitchener.
1899:	The condominium period of joint rule by Great Britain and Egypt begins.
1955:	The First Sudanese Civil War begins, pitting rebels from southern Sudan against the incoming government in Khartoum.
1956:	Sudan becomes an independent country.
1964:	Sudanese students, civil servants, and trade unionists protest against the Abbud government. Riots break out in Khartoum and other cities.
1965:	New elections are held, and a coalition government led by Muhammad Ahmed Mahjub is elected.
1966:	Mahjub is forced to step down, and Sadiq al-Mahdi takes power.
1967:	Mahdi coalition government collapses, and Mahjub returns to power as prime minister.

1969:	Jaafar al-Nimeri takes over the government.
1972:	Southern Sudan becomes autonomous under the Addis Ababa agreement, and much of the fighting ends.
1973:	Sudan's first constitution is adopted.
1983:	President Nimeri declares *Sharia* to be the law of Sudan, and the civil war resumes after a 10-year break.
1985:	Coup against Nimeri leaves military government in charge.
1986:	Sadiq al-Mahdi forms coalition government.
1989:	A military coup planned by Hassan al-Turabi, leader of the National Islamic Front, is carried out by General Omar al-Bashir; Bashir imposes martial law in the country.
1993:	Bashir is elected president of Sudan.
1998:	The United States destroys a pharmaceutical factory suspected of making chemical weapons in Khartoum.
2000:	Bashir is reelected to a second five-year term with 86 percent of the vote in an election widely condemned as rigged.
2003:	Armed conflict breaks out in the Darfur region of western Sudan.
2005:	A peace agreement is signed allowing an elected government for the South, with an option for it to vote for independence after six years.
2006:	Sudan refuses to allow UN peacekeeping troops to enter the country and assist in ending the Darfur conflict.
2007:	The United Nations estimates that more than 400,000 people have been killed in Darfur.
2009:	In March, the International Criminal Court issues an arrest warrant for President Bashir, accusing him of war crimes and crimes against humanity. Sudan's government refuses to respond to the warrant.
2011:	In January, more than 90 percent of southern Sudanese voted for independence in a referendum; on July 9, the Republic of South Sudan became an independent state.
2012:	In March, South Sudanese forces seize the Heglig oil fields, which are claimed by both Sudan and Southern Sudan.

FURTHER READING/INTERNET RESOURCES

Cockett, Richard. *Sudan: Darfur and the Failure of an African State*. New Haven, Conn.: Yale University Press, 2010.

Collins, Robert O. *A History of Modern Sudan*. New York: Cambridge University Press, 2008.

Jok Madut Jok. *Sudan: Race, Religion and Violence*. Oxford, UK: Oneworld Publications, 2007.

Natsios, Andrew S. *Sudan, South Sudan, and Darfur: What Everyone Needs to Know*. New York: Oxford University Press, 2012.

Snyder, Gail. *Sudan*. Philadelphia: Mason Crest, 2010.

Travel Information

http://www.lonelyplanet.com/sudan
http://www.worldtravelguide.net/sudan
http://www.state.gov/r/pa/ei/bgn/5424.htm

History and Geography

http://www.sudan.net/history.php
http://www.pbs.org/wnet/wideangle/episodes/heart-of-darfur/history-of-sudan/582/
http://www.zum.de/whkmla/region/northafrica/xsudan.html

Economic and Political Information

http://www.sudanembassy.org
https://www.cia.gov/library/publications/the-world-factbook/geos/od.html
https://www.cia.gov/library/publications/the-world-factbook/geos/su.html

Culture and Festivals

http://www.sudan.net
http://sudanartists.org
http://www.m-huether.de/sudan/sudart/

Publisher's Note: The websites listed on this page were active at the time of publication. The publisher is not responsible for websites that have changed their address or discontinued operation since the date of publication. The publisher reviews and updates the websites each time the book is reprinted.

Embassy of the Republic of Sudan
2210 Massachusetts Ave. NW
Washington, DC 20008
Tel: (202) 338-8565
Fax: (202) 667-2406
Email: info@sudanembassy.org

U.S. Department of State (travel advisories)
2201 C St. NW
Washington, DC 20520
Phone: (202) 647-5225
Fax: (202) 647-3000
Website: http://travel.state.gov

Government of Southern Sudan
Mission to the USA
1233 20th Street N.W., Suite 602
Washington, DC 20036
Phone: 202-293-7940
Fax: 202-293-7941
Website: http://www.gossmission.org

INDEX

Numbers in ***bold italic*** refer to captions.

CONTRIBUTORS/PICTURE CREDITS

Professor Robert I. Rotberg is Director of the Program on Intrastate Conflict and Conflict Resolution at the Kennedy School, Harvard University, and President of the World Peace Foundation. He is the author of a number of books and articles on Africa, including *A Political History of Tropical Africa* and *Ending Autocracy, Enabling Democracy: The Tribulations of Southern Africa*.

Dorothy Kavanaugh is a freelance writer who lives near Philadelphia. She holds a bachelor's degree in elementary education from Bryn Mawr College. Books she has written for young adults include *Religions of Africa* (Mason Crest, 2007.)